Divir

A Biblical and Metaphysical Perspective

Lorenzo A. Daughtry-Chambers

ISBN: 9798306176864

DEDICATION

To Sarah and Danielle thank you for helping me get it together and staying with me along the way.

Table of Contents

Introduction: Why Systems Matter

From the stars in the heavens to the cells in our bodies, God's creation reflects order and intentionality. This order is built on systems—interdependent parts working together for a common purpose. Systems are not just functional; they are sacred. They reveal God's nature as a God of order, not chaos.

When we fail to implement systems in our lives, we fall into disorder, frustration, and missed potential. Conversely, when we align our lives with divine systems, we position ourselves for success, blessing, and fulfillment.

This book explores how God's systems operate both biblically and metaphysically, offering practical insights to build systems for every area of your life: finances, health, communication, relationships, and spiritual growth. By the end, you will have a clear understanding of how to partner with God to create lasting change and live in divine alignment.

CHAPTER 1: GOD OF ORDER, GOD OF SYSTEMS

"For God is a God not of disorder but of peace."

(1 Corinthians 14:33, NRSV)

Order is a reflection of God's character. It is not an accident or afterthought but a deliberate expression of His divine nature. From the very beginning of creation, God reveals Himself as a master of systems—bringing light to darkness, order to chaos, and life to emptiness. His systems are the foundation of creation, and they remain the framework for how we thrive in every aspect of life.

This chapter explores God's systems as revealed in Scripture, showing how they serve as a model for establishing order in our own lives. By aligning with divine systems, we can experience the peace and abundance God desires for us.

God's Design Reflects Systems

The first chapter of Genesis opens with a world in chaos:

"The earth was a formless void and darkness covered the face of the deep, while a wind from God swept over the face of the waters" (Genesis 1:2, NRSV).

But God did not leave the earth in disarray. Over the next six days, He worked systematically, bringing structure and purpose to creation:

1. **Day One:**
   "Then God said, 'Let there be light'; and there was light. And God saw that the light was good; and God separated the light from the darkness. God called the light Day, and the darkness he called Night. And there was evening and there was morning, the first day" (Genesis 1:3-5, NRSV).

2. **Day Two:**
   "And God said, 'Let there be a dome in the midst of the waters, and let it separate the waters from the waters.' So God made the dome and separated the waters that were under the dome from the waters that were above the dome. And it was so. God called the dome Sky. And there was evening and there was morning, the second day" (Genesis 1:6-8, NRSV).

3. **Day Three:**
   "And God said, 'Let the waters under the sky be gathered together into one place, and let the dry land appear.' And it was so. God called the dry land Earth, and the waters that were gathered together he called Seas. And God saw that it was good. Then God said, 'Let the earth put forth vegetation: plants yielding seed, and fruit trees of every kind on earth that bear fruit with the seed in it.' And it was so" (Genesis 1:9-11, NRSV).

This deliberate process continued until God completed creation, declaring it "very good" on the sixth day (Genesis 1:31). The seventh day introduced the system of Sabbath—a divine rhythm of rest.

The Natural World as a System

Beyond the creation story, the natural world reflects God's systems. Consider the following:

- The cycle of day and night sustains life on earth.
- Seasons follow a predictable pattern—winter gives way to spring, spring to summer, and summer to autumn.
- The water cycle moves moisture through evaporation, condensation, and precipitation, replenishing the earth.
- The human body functions through interconnected systems: circulatory, respiratory, and digestive systems work in harmony to sustain life.

The psalmist captures this truth beautifully:

"The heavens are telling the glory of God; and the firmament proclaims his handiwork. Day to day pours forth speech, and night to night declares knowledge" (Psalm 19:1-2, NRSV).

If creation itself depends on systems to function, how much more should our lives?

Biblical Examples of Systems

1. The Tabernacle: A System for Worship

God's instructions for the Tabernacle in Exodus are a striking example of His order and precision:

"And have them make me a sanctuary, so that I may dwell among them. In accordance with all that I show you concerning the pattern of the tabernacle and of all its furniture, so you shall make it" (Exodus 25:8-9, NRSV).

The Tabernacle wasn't simply a place of worship; it was a system designed to teach reverence and holiness. Each part—from the altar to the Ark of the Covenant—served a specific purpose. The Tabernacle's structure demonstrated how to approach God in a systematic, meaningful way.

2. The Law: A System for Justice and Holiness

When God gave the Israelites the Law, He established a system for a just and holy society.

"You must observe them diligently, for this will show your wisdom and discernment to the peoples, who, when they hear all these statutes, will say, 'Surely this great nation is a wise and discerning people!'" (Deuteronomy 4:6, NRSV).

The commandments governed everything from worship to relationships and even economic practices. This system ensured that the people could live in harmony with God and one another.

3. The Early Church: A System for Community

The early church thrived because it embraced a system of fellowship, teaching, and mutual care:

"They devoted themselves to the apostles' teaching and fellowship, to the breaking of bread and the prayers. Awe came upon everyone, because many wonders and signs were being done by the apostles. All who believed were together and had all things in common" (Acts 2:42-44, NRSV).

This system allowed the church to grow spiritually and practically, meeting the needs of its members and spreading the gospel.

Metaphysical Insights into Systems

1. Energy Flows Through Systems

In nature, energy flows efficiently when guided by systems. For example, a river flows smoothly when its banks provide direction. Without structure, the water would spread chaotically, losing its power and purpose.

This principle applies to our lives as well. Systems create pathways for our energy, resources, and efforts to flow effectively. Without systems, chaos ensues.

2. Chaos is the Absence of Alignment

Disorder arises when elements are out of alignment with their purpose. Systems restore harmony by organizing resources and actions around a central goal. As Albert Einstein observed:

"Out of clutter, find simplicity. From discord, find harmony. In the middle of difficulty lies opportunity."

When we create systems in our lives, we align ourselves with God's design and open the door for peace and productivity.

Reflection: Finding God's Order in Your Life

Take a moment to evaluate your own life. Where do you see God's order and systems at work? Perhaps in the way you manage your time, care for your health, or steward your finances.

Now consider the areas where chaos reigns. Are you struggling to maintain relationships? Is your spiritual life inconsistent? These areas may be calling for systems to bring alignment and peace.

Action Steps for Chapter 1

1. **Identify Chaos:**
   Write down one area of your life that feels disorganized or overwhelming.

2. **Create a Simple System:**
   Reflect on God's systems in creation or Scripture for inspiration. For example:

   - Establish a morning routine for prayer and reflection.
   - Set up a weekly budget for financial peace.

- Plan consistent family time to strengthen relationships.

3. **Commit to One Change:**
   Start small. Implement one system this week and evaluate its impact.

Conclusion: Aligning with Divine Order

God's systems are designed to bring peace, growth, and abundance. By aligning our lives with His order, we reflect His character and experience the fullness of His blessings.

"Commit your way to the Lord; trust in him, and he will act" (Psalm 37:5, NRSV).

As we continue this journey, let us embrace the systems God has modeled for us, knowing that His order leads to life and peace.

CHAPTER 2: THE ANATOMY OF A SYSTEM

"But all things should be done decently and in order."

(1 Corinthians 14:40, NRSV)

God's systems are intentional, structured, and purpose-driven. They are not haphazard but designed to fulfill a specific purpose in creation and in our lives. To implement systems effectively, we must understand their anatomy—what makes a system functional and successful.

In this chapter, we will explore the components of a system, examine their role in God's design, and reflect on how to build systems in our own lives.

What is a System?

A system is a set of interrelated parts that work together to achieve a specific purpose. Systems require three essential components:

1. **Structure:** The framework or design that organizes the system.

2. **Function:** The purpose or goal the system is designed to achieve.

3. **Process:** The method or steps that enable the system to operate.

For example, consider the respiratory system in the human body:

- The **structure** includes the lungs, trachea, and diaphragm.
- The **function** is to bring oxygen into the body and remove carbon dioxide.
- The **process** involves inhaling, oxygen exchange, and exhaling.

When any part of the system is missing or malfunctioning, the system as a whole suffers.

God's Systems in Creation

Scripture reveals that God's systems reflect these three components —structure, function, and process. Let's examine a few examples.

1. Creation's Systems

Genesis 1 demonstrates how God implemented systems to sustain life:

- **Structure:** God created the heavens, the earth, and the seas as the framework for life.
  "God said, 'Let the waters under the sky be gathered together into one place, and let the dry land appear.' And it was so" (Genesis 1:9, NRSV).
- **Function:** These structures support living organisms, providing a habitat for plants, animals, and humans.
- **Process:** God established processes such as the water cycle, photosynthesis, and reproduction to sustain creation.

"Then God said, 'Let the earth put forth vegetation: plants yielding seed, and fruit trees of every kind on earth that bear fruit with the seed in it.' And it was so" (Genesis 1:11, NRSV).

The interdependence of these systems demonstrates God's wisdom and intentionality.

2. The Tabernacle's System

The Tabernacle is another example of a divinely designed system.

- **Structure:** The Tabernacle had specific dimensions and materials (Exodus 26:1-37). The outer court, Holy Place, and Holy of Holies were arranged with precision.

- **Function:** The Tabernacle was designed as a meeting place between God and His people.
"Let them make me a sanctuary, so that I may dwell among them" (Exodus 25:8, NRSV).

- **Process:** The priests followed a detailed process of sacrifices, offerings, and rituals to maintain the system and ensure that it operated effectively (Leviticus 1-7).

Each part of the Tabernacle served a purpose, working together to create a sacred system of worship.

3. The Body of Christ

The Church, often called the Body of Christ, operates as a spiritual system.

- **Structure:** The Church is made up of many members, each with unique roles and gifts.
"For just as the body is one and has many members, and all the members of the body, though many, are one body, so it is with Christ" (1 Corinthians 12:12, NRSV).

- **Function:** The Church's purpose is to glorify God, spread the gospel, and care for one another.
  "Go therefore and make disciples of all nations" (Matthew 28:19, NRSV).

- **Process:** This system relies on prayer, teaching, fellowship, and service to fulfill its mission.

"They devoted themselves to the apostles' teaching and fellowship, to the breaking of bread and the prayers" (Acts 2:42, NRSV).

Why Systems Fail

Even the best-designed systems can fail if one or more components are neglected. Here are some common reasons systems break down:

1. **Lack of Structure:** Without clear boundaries and organization, chaos takes over. For example, finances without a budget often lead to overspending and debt.

2. **Unclear Purpose:** A system without a clear function lacks direction and motivation.

3. **Broken Processes:** Inefficient or neglected processes prevent systems from operating effectively.

Jesus emphasized the importance of counting the cost and planning carefully:

"For which of you, intending to build a tower, does not first sit down and estimate the cost, to see whether he has enough to complete it?" (Luke 14:28, NRSV).

If we want to build systems that succeed, we must be intentional about their design and maintenance.

Reflection: Evaluating Your Systems

Take a moment to reflect on the systems in your life. Ask yourself:

1. **What systems are working well?**
   - Do you have a morning routine that supports your spiritual growth?
   - Is your financial system (e.g., budgeting, saving) bringing you peace?
2. **What systems are missing or broken?**
   - Are your health habits inconsistent?
   - Do you lack a system for maintaining healthy relationships or communication?
3. **How can you improve these systems?**
   - What structural changes are needed?
   - How can you clarify the purpose of this system?
   - What processes can you implement or refine?

Action Steps for Chapter 2

1. **Identify One Area for Improvement:**
   Write down one area of your life that feels disorganized or ineffective.
2. **Design a System:**
   Using the framework of structure, function, and process, outline a simple system to address this area. For example:
   - **Health System:**
     - Structure: Create a weekly meal plan and schedule exercise.

- Function: Improve physical health and energy levels.
- Process: Shop for groceries on Sunday, prepare meals in advance, and exercise three times per week.

3. **Commit to the Process:**
Implement your new system for one week and evaluate its effectiveness. Adjust as needed to ensure it serves its purpose.

Conclusion: Partnering with God to Build Systems

God's systems in creation, worship, and the Church reveal His wisdom and intentionality. As His children, we are called to model this order in our own lives. When we design systems with structure, purpose, and process, we align ourselves with His divine nature and create a foundation for growth and peace.

"Commit your work to the Lord, and your plans will be established" (Proverbs 16:3, NRSV).

In the next chapter, we will explore how to create systems for specific areas of life—finances, health, communication, and relationships—so that we can experience the fullness of God's blessings.

CHAPTER 3: FINANCIAL SYSTEMS – STEWARDSHIP AND ABUNDANCE

"Whoever is faithful in a very little is faithful also in much; and whoever is dishonest in a very little is dishonest also in much."

(Luke 16:10, NRSV)

God's Word is clear: financial stewardship is a spiritual responsibility. Money is not merely a tool for survival or success; it is a resource entrusted to us by God to manage wisely for His glory and our good. When we honor God with our finances through intentional systems, we unlock the blessings of abundance, peace, and freedom.

In this chapter, we will explore the biblical principles of stewardship, examine the dangers of financial chaos, and learn how to create systems that align with God's purposes for our finances.

Biblical Principles of Financial Stewardship

1. God Owns It All

The foundation of financial stewardship is understanding that everything we have belongs to God.

"The earth is the Lord's and all that is in it, the world, and those who live in it" (Psalm 24:1, NRSV).

We are not owners but stewards—managers of resources entrusted to us by God. This perspective shifts our mindset from self-centered accumulation to God-centered generosity.

2. Tithing: Honoring God First

Tithing is a system established by God to teach His people trust and obedience.

"Bring the full tithe into the storehouse, so that there may be food in my house, and thus put me to the test, says the Lord of hosts; see if I will not open the windows of heaven for you and pour down for you an overflowing blessing" (Malachi 3:10, NRSV).

When we prioritize giving to God first, we invite His provision and protection over our finances.

3. Avoiding Debt

Debt is a form of financial bondage that limits our ability to serve God and others.

"The rich rule over the poor, and the borrower is the slave of the lender" (Proverbs 22:7, NRSV).

While some debt may be necessary for significant investments like education or housing, living within our means and avoiding unnecessary debt are critical components of financial stewardship.

4. Generosity as a Way of Life

God calls us to use our resources to bless others, reflecting His generosity.

"Give, and it will be given to you. A good measure, pressed down, shaken together, running over, will be put into your lap; for the measure you give will be the measure you get back" (Luke 6:38, NRSV).

Generosity is not about the size of the gift but the heart behind it. It is a reflection of our trust in God's provision.

The Dangers of Financial Chaos

Without systems, our finances can quickly spiral into disorder, leading to stress, anxiety, and even spiritual consequences. Here are some common pitfalls of financial mismanagement:

1. **Impulsive Spending:** Without a budget, it's easy to spend beyond our means, creating unnecessary debt.

2. **Lack of Savings:** Emergencies or unexpected expenses can leave us vulnerable without a plan for savings.

3. **Neglecting Giving:** Without intentionality, we may overlook the importance of giving as an act of worship and trust.

4. **Disorganization:** Missed payments, forgotten bills, and disorganized records create chaos and strain relationships.

Paul's admonition to the Corinthians is a reminder of the importance of order:

"For God is a God not of disorder but of peace" (1 Corinthians 14:33, NRSV).

Financial systems bring peace by providing clarity, discipline, and purpose.

Creating a Financial System

Step 1: Assess Your Current Situation

Before creating a financial system, it's essential to understand where you stand. Write down:

- Your total income (monthly or yearly).
- Your total expenses, including fixed costs (rent, utilities) and variable costs (groceries, entertainment).

- Any outstanding debts or obligations.

Step 2: Set Financial Goals

Align your goals with biblical principles. Examples include:

- **Short-Term Goals:** Save $1,000 for an emergency fund, pay off a credit card, or tithe consistently.
- **Long-Term Goals:** Save for a home, plan for retirement, or create a fund for education or missions.

"The plans of the diligent lead surely to abundance, but everyone who is hasty comes only to want" (Proverbs 21:5, NRSV).

Step 3: Create a Budget

A budget is a practical tool for managing your money. Use the following categories:

- **Tithing and Giving (10%):** Start by honoring God with the first portion of your income.
- **Savings (10-20%):** Build an emergency fund and save for future goals.
- **Expenses (70-80%):** Allocate funds for housing, food, transportation, and other needs.

Tools like budgeting apps or spreadsheets can help simplify this process.

Step 4: Automate Your Systems

Automating your finances reduces stress and ensures consistency. Examples include:

- Setting up automatic transfers for tithes and savings.

- Scheduling bill payments to avoid late fees.

"Let all things be done decently and in order" (1 Corinthians 14:40, NRSV).

Step 5: Review and Adjust

Your financial system should be dynamic, adapting to changes in income, expenses, or goals. Regularly review your budget and adjust as needed.

Reflection: Are Your Finances in Order?

Take a moment to evaluate your financial habits. Ask yourself:

1. **Am I honoring God with my finances?**
2. **Do I have a system for budgeting, saving, and giving?**
3. **What steps can I take to improve my financial stewardship?**

Action Steps for Chapter 3

1. **Create a Budget:**
   Write down your income and expenses. Allocate percentages for tithing, saving, and spending.
2. **Start Small:**
   - Begin tithing with a consistent amount, even if it's not yet 10%.
   - Save \$50–\$100 a month to build an emergency fund.
3. **Eliminate Waste:**
   Identify one unnecessary expense and redirect that money toward savings or giving.

4. **Pray Over Your Finances:**
   Commit your financial goals to God, asking for wisdom and discipline.

Conclusion: Faithful Stewards of God's Resources

Financial systems are not just practical tools; they are spiritual disciplines. When we align our finances with God's principles, we demonstrate faithfulness, gratitude, and trust in His provision.

"Do not store up for yourselves treasures on earth, where moth and rust consume and where thieves break in and steal; but store up for yourselves treasures in heaven, where neither moth nor rust consumes and where thieves do not break in and steal. For where your treasure is, there your heart will be also" (Matthew 6:19-21, NRSV).

As you implement your financial system, remember that stewardship is about more than managing money—it's about managing your heart. In the next chapter, we will explore how to build systems for health and well-being, honoring God with our bodies and minds.

CHAPTER 4: HEALTH AND WELL-BEING SYSTEMS – HONORING GOD WITH YOUR BODY

"Do you not know that your body is a temple of the Holy Spirit within you, which you have from God, and that you are not your own?"

(1 Corinthians 6:19, NRSV)

Our health is a divine trust. God created our bodies with care and purpose, and He calls us to steward them as vessels for His glory. Yet, in the busyness of life, we often neglect the physical, mental, and emotional systems that sustain us. The Bible is filled with wisdom about how to care for our bodies and minds, teaching us that well-being is not a luxury but a responsibility.

In this chapter, we will examine the biblical principles of health, identify the dangers of neglecting well-being, and learn how to implement practical systems for a balanced and thriving life.

Biblical Principles of Health and Well-Being

1. Your Body is a Temple

Paul reminds us that our bodies are sacred, designed to house the Holy Spirit.

"So glorify God in your body" (1 Corinthians 6:20, NRSV).

Caring for our physical health is not vanity; it is an act of worship. When we nourish and strengthen our bodies, we honor the Creator who designed them.

2. Rest is Holy

God modeled the importance of rest by instituting the Sabbath.

"Six days you shall labor and do all your work. But the seventh day is a sabbath to the Lord your God; you shall not do any work" (Exodus 20:9-10, NRSV).

Rest is essential for renewal, both physically and spiritually. It is a system God put in place to sustain us.

3. Moderation and Discipline

The Bible warns against both excess and neglect.

"Do not get drunk with wine, for that is debauchery; but be filled with the Spirit" (Ephesians 5:18, NRSV).

Discipline in our habits—whether eating, exercising, or sleeping—helps us maintain balance and focus on God's purposes.

4. Mental and Emotional Health Matters

God cares about our minds as much as our bodies.

"Do not worry about anything, but in everything by prayer and supplication with thanksgiving let your requests be made known to

God. And the peace of God, which surpasses all understanding, will guard your hearts and your minds in Christ Jesus" (Philippians 4:6-7, NRSV).

A sound mind is a gift from God, and nurturing it through prayer, reflection, and healthy practices is essential for holistic well-being.

The Dangers of Neglecting Health

When we neglect our health, we risk not only physical consequences but also spiritual and emotional struggles. Common pitfalls include:

1. **Burnout:** Overworking without rest can lead to exhaustion and diminished productivity.
2. **Poor Nutrition:** Neglecting proper nutrition weakens the body and impairs focus.
3. **Lack of Exercise:** A sedentary lifestyle contributes to chronic illnesses and reduced energy.
4. **Mental Strain:** Stress and anxiety, when unchecked, can overwhelm our peace and purpose.

Proverbs offers a warning:

"A tranquil mind gives life to the flesh, but passion makes the bones rot" (Proverbs 14:30, NRSV).

Neglecting health affects every area of life, reducing our ability to serve God and others effectively.

Creating a Health and Well-Being System

Step 1: Establish Priorities

Reflect on what areas of your health need attention—physical, mental, or emotional. Ask yourself:

- Am I getting enough sleep?

- Do I eat foods that nourish my body?
- Do I take time to rest and reflect?
- Am I managing stress effectively?

Step 2: Develop a Daily Rhythm

God designed the world with rhythms of day and night, work and rest. Create a personal rhythm that incorporates:

- **Rest:** Aim for 7-9 hours of sleep per night.
- **Nourishment:** Plan balanced meals with whole foods.
- **Movement:** Commit to at least 30 minutes of physical activity daily.
- **Reflection:** Spend time in prayer, journaling, or meditation to care for your mind and spirit.

Step 3: Plan for Sabbath Rest

Dedicate one day a week to intentional rest and worship. Use this time to:

- Disconnect from work and technology.
- Spend time with family or in nature.
- Reflect on God's goodness and recharge your spirit.

"Come to me, all you that are weary and are carrying heavy burdens, and I will give you rest" (Matthew 11:28, NRSV).

Step 4: Address Mental Health Proactively

Create systems to manage stress and promote mental well-being:

- Practice gratitude daily by writing down three things you're thankful for.
- Seek counsel or therapy when needed—God often works through wise counselors.
- Meditate on God's promises to replace worry with peace.

"You will keep in perfect peace those whose minds are stayed on you, because they trust in you" (Isaiah 26:3, NRSV).

Reflection: Are You Honoring God with Your Health?

Take a moment to reflect on your health habits. Ask yourself:

1. **Am I treating my body as a temple of the Holy Spirit?**
2. **Do I have a healthy rhythm of work, rest, and worship?**
3. **What steps can I take to improve my physical, mental, and emotional well-being?**

Action Steps for Chapter 4

1. **Assess Your Habits:**
   Write down your current practices in the areas of sleep, nutrition, exercise, and mental health. Identify one area to improve.
2. **Create a Health Plan:**
   Design a simple system to support your well-being. For example:
   - Set a bedtime and wake-up time to ensure consistent rest.
   - Plan your meals for the week, focusing on balance and moderation.
   - Schedule specific times for exercise and reflection.

3. **Start Small and Stay Consistent:**
   Begin with one habit, such as walking for 20 minutes a day or cutting out sugary drinks. Build momentum through consistency.

4. **Involve God in Your Journey:**
   Pray for wisdom, strength, and discipline as you care for your health.

Conclusion: Stewardship of the Body

Caring for your health is a spiritual act of stewardship. When you honor God with your body, mind, and emotions, you position yourself to live a life of greater purpose and effectiveness. Remember: your well-being is not just for your benefit—it is also for God's glory and the service of others.

"Beloved, I pray that all may go well with you and that you may be in good health, just as it is well with your soul" (3 John 1:2, NRSV).

In the next chapter, we will explore systems for communication, examining how to speak life, build relationships, and honor God with our words.

CHAPTER 5: COMMUNICATION SYSTEMS – SPEAKING LIFE AND BUILDING CONNECTIONS

"Let no evil talk come out of your mouths, but only what is useful for building up, as there is need, so that your words may give grace to those who hear."

(Ephesians 4:29, NRSV)

Words have power. The Bible tells us that life and death are in the power of the tongue (Proverbs 18:21). God Himself spoke the world into existence, demonstrating the creative potential of language. As His image-bearers, our words also have the power to build, heal, and transform—or to tear down and destroy.

In this chapter, we will explore biblical principles for communication, the importance of intentionality in our words, and how to develop systems that foster healthy and effective communication in all areas of life.

Biblical Principles of Communication

1. Words Reflect the Heart

Jesus taught that our words reveal the condition of our hearts.

"For out of the abundance of the heart the mouth speaks" (Matthew 12:34, NRSV).

If we want our communication to be life-giving, we must first allow God to transform our hearts.

2. Speak with Grace and Truth

Effective communication balances grace and truth.

"Speaking the truth in love, we must grow up in every way into him who is the head, into Christ" (Ephesians 4:15, NRSV).

Truth is necessary for growth, but grace ensures that truth is delivered in a way that builds up rather than wounds.

3. Be Quick to Listen, Slow to Speak

James gives us a timeless principle for communication:

"You must understand this, my beloved: let everyone be quick to listen, slow to speak, slow to anger; for your anger does not produce God's righteousness" (James 1:19-20, NRSV).

Listening is the foundation of healthy communication. It shows respect, fosters understanding, and prevents unnecessary conflict.

4. Avoid Gossip and Slander

The Bible repeatedly warns against the destructive nature of gossip and slander.

"A gossip goes about telling secrets, but one who is trustworthy in spirit keeps a confidence" (Proverbs 11:13, NRSV).

"Do not speak evil against one another, brothers and sisters" (James 4:11, NRSV).

Guarding our words ensures that we honor others and maintain integrity in our relationships.

The Dangers of Poor Communication

When communication lacks intentionality, it leads to misunderstandings, broken relationships, and even spiritual harm. Common pitfalls include:

1. **Misunderstanding:** Speaking without clarity or context can create confusion.
2. **Conflict:** Harsh or careless words escalate tension and hurt feelings.
3. **Neglect:** Failing to communicate consistently weakens relationships.
4. **Negativity:** Critical or pessimistic speech drains energy and damages trust.

Proverbs warns of the destructive potential of words:

"A soft answer turns away wrath, but a harsh word stirs up anger" (Proverbs 15:1, NRSV).

To avoid these pitfalls, we must develop systems that promote thoughtful, consistent, and edifying communication.

Creating a Communication System

Step 1: Prioritize Relationships

Healthy communication begins with valuing the people you interact with. Ask yourself:

- Am I intentional about staying connected with family, friends, and colleagues?
- Do I create space for meaningful conversations?
- Do I listen actively and empathetically?

Step 2: Develop Daily Practices

Incorporate communication habits into your daily routine:

- **Start with Prayer:** Begin each day by asking God to guide your words."Set a guard over my mouth, O Lord; keep watch over the door of my lips" (Psalm 141:3, NRSV).

- **Send Encouragement:** Text or call someone with an encouraging word.

- **Practice Gratitude:** Speak words of appreciation to those around you.

Step 3: Create Boundaries for Difficult Conversations

Not all conversations are easy. For challenging topics, establish boundaries to keep communication respectful and productive:

- Choose a neutral time and place.

- Focus on the issue, not the person.

- Use "I" statements (e.g., "I feel" instead of "You always”).

- Commit to listening without interrupting.

"If it is possible, so far as it depends on you, live peaceably with all" (Romans 12:18, NRSV).

Step 4: Schedule Regular Check-Ins

Consistency strengthens communication. Whether it’s a weekly family meeting, a monthly call with a friend, or daily updates with your spouse, set aside intentional time to connect.

Step 5: Use Technology Wisely

Leverage technology to support communication, but don't let it replace personal connection. For example:

- Use calendars and reminders to remember birthdays or important dates.
- Schedule virtual meetings with loved ones who live far away.

Reflection: Are Your Words Life-Giving?

Take a moment to evaluate your communication habits. Ask yourself:

1. **Do my words build others up or tear them down?**

2. **Am I intentional about listening and understanding others?**

3. **What steps can I take to improve my communication in key relationships?**

Action Steps for Chapter 5

1. **Identify Communication Gaps:**
   Write down three relationships where communication could be improved.

2. **Start a Communication Habit:**
   Choose one daily habit to practice, such as:

   - Writing a note of encouragement.

   - Spending 10 minutes listening without distractions.

   - Praying for someone before speaking with them.

3. **Commit to One Improvement:**
   Focus on one specific area to strengthen, such as active

listening, reducing negativity, or addressing conflicts constructively.

4. **Ask for Feedback:**
   Invite a trusted person to share their perspective on your communication style and areas for growth.

Conclusion: Speaking Life and Building Connections

Communication is not just a skill; it is a reflection of God's character in us. When we use our words to build up, encourage, and heal, we reflect the love and grace of Christ. By implementing systems that prioritize intentionality, clarity, and consistency, we can strengthen our relationships and honor God with our speech.

"Let the words of my mouth and the meditation of my heart be acceptable to you, O Lord, my rock and my redeemer" (Psalm 19:14, NRSV).

In the next chapter, we will explore how to develop systems for relationships, focusing on cultivating covenant connections and fostering mutual support.

CHAPTER 6: RELATIONSHIP SYSTEMS – BUILDING COVENANT CONNECTIONS

"Two are better than one, because they have a good reward for their toil. For if they fall, one will lift up the other; but woe to one who is alone and falls and does not have another to help."

(Ecclesiastes 4:9-10, NRSV)

Relationships are at the heart of God's design for humanity. From the beginning, God declared that it was "not good" for man to be alone (Genesis 2:18). Healthy relationships provide love, support, and accountability, enabling us to fulfill our purpose and glorify God.

However, like every other area of life, relationships thrive when nurtured with intentional systems. Covenant relationships—whether with family, friends, or fellow believers—require commitment, communication, and care to flourish. This chapter will explore biblical principles for building strong relationships and practical systems to strengthen the connections that matter most.

Biblical Principles of Covenant Relationships

1. Relationships Reflect God's Nature

God Himself exists in eternal relationship—Father, Son, and Holy Spirit. As image-bearers of God, we are created for connection.

"Then God said, 'Let us make humankind in our image, according to our likeness'" (Genesis 1:26, NRSV).

Our relationships are an opportunity to reflect the love, unity, and selflessness of the Trinity.

2. Covenant over Convenience

Biblical relationships are rooted in covenant, not convenience. A covenant is a sacred commitment to love and serve others, even when it's difficult.

"Therefore what God has joined together, let no one separate" (Mark 10:9, NRSV).

This principle applies not only to marriage but to friendships, family, and the body of Christ. Covenant relationships require faithfulness and perseverance.

3. Love is the Foundation

Jesus emphasized love as the defining characteristic of His followers:

"I give you a new commandment, that you love one another. Just as I have loved you, you also should love one another" (John 13:34, NRSV).

Biblical love is sacrificial and action-oriented, seeking the good of others before self.

4. Forgiveness is Essential

No relationship is without conflict, but forgiveness restores and strengthens broken bonds.

"Bear with one another and, if anyone has a complaint against another, forgive each other; just as the Lord has forgiven you, so you also must forgive" (Colossians 3:13, NRSV).

Without forgiveness, relationships are hindered by resentment and bitterness.

The Dangers of Neglecting Relationships

When relationships are neglected, they can become strained, distant, or even severed. Common pitfalls include:

1. **Lack of Communication:** Without consistent connection, relationships weaken over time.
2. **Unresolved Conflict:** Avoiding difficult conversations can lead to resentment and division.
3. **Self-Centeredness:** Focusing solely on personal needs undermines the mutual support that relationships provide.
4. **Busyness:** Failing to prioritize relationships due to work or other obligations creates disconnection.

Proverbs warns of the consequences of relational neglect:

"A friend loves at all times, and kinsfolk are born to share adversity" (Proverbs 17:17, NRSV).

Healthy relationships require time, effort, and intentionality.

Creating a Relationship System

Step 1: Identify Your Core Relationships

Start by reflecting on the key relationships in your life. Consider:

- **Family:** Spouse, children, parents, and extended family.
- **Friends:** Close companions who provide encouragement and accountability.
- **Community:** Fellow believers or colleagues who support and challenge you.

Make a list of these relationships and evaluate their current state. Are they thriving, strained, or in need of attention?

Step 2: Prioritize Quality Time

Relationships are strengthened through shared experiences and meaningful conversations. Build intentional time into your schedule for:

- **Family Time:** Weekly dinners, game nights, or outings.
- **Friendships:** Regular check-ins via phone, video calls, or in-person visits.
- **Community Involvement:** Serving together in ministry or participating in small groups.

"And let us consider how to provoke one another to love and good deeds, not neglecting to meet together, as is the habit of some, but encouraging one another" (Hebrews 10:24-25, NRSV).

Step 3: Address Conflict Proactively

Conflict is inevitable, but it doesn't have to damage relationships. Use the following system for resolving disagreements:

1. **Pray for Guidance:** Ask God to give you wisdom and humility.

2. **Speak the Truth in Love:** Share your feelings honestly and respectfully.

3. **Listen Actively:** Seek to understand the other person's perspective without interrupting.

4. **Seek Reconciliation:** Focus on finding solutions that restore harmony.

"If another member of the church sins against you, go and point out the fault when the two of you are alone. If the member listens to you, you have regained that one" (Matthew 18:15, NRSV).

Step 4: Create Boundaries for Healthy Relationships

Boundaries protect relationships by ensuring mutual respect and understanding. Examples include:

- Setting limits on time or energy for toxic or draining relationships.

- Communicating clearly about expectations and needs.

- Protecting your marriage by prioritizing your spouse over other commitments.

"Do not be deceived: 'Bad company ruins good morals'" (1 Corinthians 15:33, NRSV).

Step 5: Celebrate and Invest in Relationships

Strong relationships require intentional investment. Celebrate milestones, express gratitude, and continually look for ways to serve and encourage those around you.

Reflection: How Are Your Relationships?

Take a moment to evaluate your relationships. Ask yourself:

1. **Am I investing time and energy in the people who matter most?**
2. **Are there unresolved conflicts I need to address?**
3. **What steps can I take to strengthen and nurture my relationships?**

Action Steps for Chapter 6

1. **Evaluate Your Key Relationships:**
   Write down the names of 5-10 people who are most important in your life. Reflect on how you can prioritize and strengthen these connections.
2. **Schedule Quality Time:**
   Plan at least one meaningful interaction this week with a family member, friend, or community member.
3. **Address One Conflict:**
   Identify a relationship where conflict exists. Take the first step toward resolution by reaching out with humility and grace.
4. **Express Gratitude:**
   Write a note, make a call, or have a conversation to thank someone who has impacted your life.

Conclusion: Building Covenant Connections

Relationships are a sacred gift, designed by God to support, challenge, and refine us. When we build systems to nurture these connections, we reflect the covenantal love of God and create a foundation for mutual growth and encouragement.

"Above all, maintain constant love for one another, for love covers a multitude of sins" (1 Peter 4:8, NRSV).

In the next chapter, we will explore spiritual systems, focusing on how disciplines like prayer, fasting, and worship help us align with God's purposes and grow in faith.

Chapter 7: Spiritual Systems – Aligning with the Divine

"Discipline yourselves for the purpose of godliness."

(1 Timothy 4:7b, NRSV)

Spiritual growth is not accidental—it is intentional. God invites us into a deeper relationship with Him through disciplines and practices that align our hearts, minds, and spirits with His will. These spiritual systems—prayer, fasting, worship, and Scripture study—are not empty rituals but pathways to transformation and intimacy with God.

In this chapter, we will explore how to build spiritual systems that cultivate discipline, foster alignment with God's purposes, and position us to live in His power and presence.

Biblical Principles of Spiritual Systems

1. God is a God of Relationship

From the Garden of Eden to the Great Commission, God's desire has always been relationship with His people.

"I will take you as my people, and I will be your God" (Exodus 6:7a, NRSV).

Spiritual systems are not about earning God's favor; they are tools for deepening our connection with Him.

2. Discipline Leads to Godliness

Paul emphasized the importance of spiritual discipline for growth:

"Train yourselves in godliness, for while physical training is of some value, godliness is valuable in every way, holding promise for both the present life and the life to come" (1 Timothy 4:7b-8, NRSV).

Like an athlete preparing for competition, we must train consistently to grow spiritually.

3. Abide in Christ

Jesus taught that spiritual fruitfulness comes from abiding in Him:

"Abide in me as I abide in you. Just as the branch cannot bear fruit by itself unless it abides in the vine, neither can you unless you abide in me" (John 15:4, NRSV).

Spiritual systems help us remain connected to the true source of life and strength.

4. Prayer and Worship Transform Us

Through prayer and worship, we align our hearts with God's will and experience His transforming power.

"Do not worry about anything, but in everything by prayer and supplication with thanksgiving let your requests be made known to God. And the peace of God, which surpasses all understanding, will guard your hearts and your minds in Christ Jesus" (Philippians 4:6-7, NRSV).

The Dangers of Spiritual Neglect

When we neglect spiritual disciplines, we risk:

1. **Drifting Away from God:** Without consistent connection, our relationship with God can become distant.

2. **Weakness in Temptation:** Spiritual systems strengthen our faith, making us less vulnerable to sin.

3. **Lack of Peace:** Neglecting prayer, worship, and Scripture leaves us unanchored in life's storms.

4. **Missed Purpose:** Without alignment with God, we may pursue paths that lead to frustration instead of fulfillment.

Jesus warned His disciples of the need for vigilance and prayer:

"Keep awake and pray that you may not come into the time of trial; the spirit indeed is willing, but the flesh is weak" (Mark 14:38, NRSV).

Spiritual neglect not only weakens us but distances us from the abundant life God desires for us.

Building a Spiritual System

Step 1: Establish a Daily Rhythm with God

Daily time with God anchors your spiritual life. Your rhythm may include:

- **Prayer:** Begin and end each day in prayer."Very early in the morning, while it was still dark, he got up and went out to a deserted place, and there he prayed" (Mark 1:35, NRSV).

- **Scripture Reading:** Spend time meditating on God's Word."Your word is a lamp to my feet and a light to my path" (Psalm 119:105, NRSV).

- **Worship:** Incorporate music, gratitude, or silence to connect with God.

Step 2: Set Weekly Practices

Dedicate specific days to deepen your spiritual practices:

- **Sabbath Rest:** Observe a day of rest and worship to honor God."Remember the sabbath day, and keep it holy" (Exodus 20:8, NRSV).

- **Fasting:** Fast regularly to focus on spiritual growth and dependence on God."When you fast, do not look somber as the hypocrites do" (Matthew 6:16, NRSV).

Step 3: Join a Spiritual Community

Spiritual growth thrives in the context of community:

- Participate in Bible studies or small groups.

- Engage in corporate worship regularly.

- Seek mentorship and accountability from mature believers.

"As iron sharpens iron, so one person sharpens another" (Proverbs 27:17, NRSV).

Step 4: Create a System for Reflection

Set aside time each month to evaluate your spiritual growth:

- Are you consistent in prayer, Scripture reading, and worship?

- What is God teaching you?

- How are you applying His truth in your life?

Reflection: Are You Spiritually Aligned?

Take a moment to evaluate your spiritual practices. Ask yourself:

1. **Am I spending consistent, meaningful time with God?**
2. **Do I have systems that help me stay connected to Him?**
3. **What steps can I take to strengthen my spiritual life?**

Action Steps for Chapter 7

1. **Start a Daily Quiet Time:**
   Dedicate 15–30 minutes each day for prayer, Scripture, and reflection.
2. **Choose One Weekly Discipline:**
   Commit to one additional practice, such as fasting, Sabbath rest, or journaling.
3. **Engage in Community:**
   Join a small group, prayer circle, or discipleship program to grow alongside others.
4. **Track Your Progress:**
   Use a journal to record your insights, prayers, and spiritual growth.

Conclusion: Living in Divine Alignment

Spiritual systems are not about perfection; they are about connection. As we develop rhythms of prayer, worship, and reflection, we draw closer to God and align our lives with His purposes. These systems equip us to live abundantly, serve faithfully, and bear fruit for His kingdom.

"I am the vine, you are the branches. Those who abide in me and I in them bear much fruit, because apart from me you can do nothing" (John 15:5, NRSV).

In the next chapter, we will address the obstacles to maintaining systems and explore strategies for overcoming chaos, resistance, and distractions in our journey toward order and growth.

Chapter 8: Consistency in Godly Systems

Scripture:
"Let us not grow weary in doing what is right, for we will reap at harvest time, if we do not give up." – Galatians 6:9 (NRSV)

Introduction: The Power of Consistency

Consistency is the secret ingredient to success in any system. No matter how well a system is designed, it cannot work without commitment and persistence. God's Word consistently highlights the importance of faithfulness and endurance, reminding us that transformation comes not from occasional effort but from steady, faithful action over time.

Consider the farmer who plants a field. He waters, weeds, and nurtures his crops day by day. Even though he doesn't see the harvest immediately, he knows the outcome depends on his daily care. Similarly, the systems we create—whether for our finances, health, or spiritual growth—will only bear fruit if we remain consistent.

1. The Biblical Case for Consistency

The Bible is filled with examples of individuals who reaped blessings because of their faithful commitment to God's ways:

- **Noah:**
  Noah spent decades building the ark, trusting God's plan even

when the task seemed overwhelming (Genesis 6:13-22). His obedience and persistence saved his family and preserved creation.
Lesson: Consistency in God's instructions brings protection and provision.

- **The Israelites in the Wilderness:**
God provided manna daily, requiring the Israelites to gather it faithfully each morning (Exodus 16:4-5). This system taught them to depend on God consistently.
Lesson: Daily trust and action sustain us.

- **Jesus in Prayer:**
Jesus modeled consistency by withdrawing to pray regularly, even amid His demanding ministry (Luke 5:16).
Lesson: Consistency in spiritual disciplines strengthens us for life's challenges.

2. Why Consistency Matters

Consistency transforms small, daily actions into lasting change. Here's why it matters:

1. **Builds Momentum:**
Every small, consistent step compounds over time, making significant progress possible.

2. **Reinforces Habits:**
Repetition strengthens neural pathways, making positive behaviors automatic.

3. **Demonstrates Faithfulness:**
Our consistent effort reflects our trust in God's promises, even when results aren't immediate.

4. **Produces Long-Term Results:**
Like planting seeds, consistent action today yields a harvest in the future (Galatians 6:9).

3. Obstacles to Consistency

Remaining faithful to systems can be challenging. Here are common obstacles and biblical strategies to overcome them:

1. **Distractions:**
   - **Example:** Martha was distracted by her tasks, missing the opportunity to sit with Jesus (Luke 10:38-42).
   - **Solution:** Prioritize what matters most and set boundaries to protect your time.

2. **Discouragement:**
   - **Example:** Elijah felt defeated after facing opposition, even though he had just seen God's power (1 Kings 19:1-10).
   - **Solution:** Seek encouragement in God's presence and His promises. Surround yourself with supportive community.

3. **Impatience:**
   - **Example:** Abraham and Sarah grew impatient waiting for God's promise, leading to detours in their journey (Genesis 16).
   - **Solution:** Trust God's timing and stay committed, knowing He is faithful.

4. **Lack of Planning:**
   - **Solution:** Use tools like trackers, schedules, and accountability partners to stay organized and intentional.

4. Practical Strategies for Staying Consistent

Consistency requires intentionality. Here are practical ways to remain faithful to your systems:

1. **Set Clear Goals:**
   Define what success looks like in each system. For example, aim to save 10% of your income each month or spend 30 minutes daily in prayer.

2. **Use Accountability:**
   Share your goals with a trusted friend, mentor, or group. Regular check-ins can keep you motivated and focused. **Scripture:** "Iron sharpens iron, and one person sharpens the wits of another" (Proverbs 27:17).

3. **Track Your Progress:**
   Use journals, apps, or printable trackers to monitor your consistency. Celebrate small wins along the way.

4. **Develop Routines:**
   Incorporate your systems into your daily or weekly schedule. For example, set a consistent time each day for prayer or financial planning.

5. **Reflect and Adjust:**
   Regularly review what's working and what isn't. Make adjustments to improve the effectiveness of your systems.

6. **Focus on God's Promises:**
   Keep Scripture at the center of your journey. Write down verses that encourage you to stay faithful and revisit them often.

Reflection Questions

1. What area of your life needs more consistency?
2. What obstacles have kept you from staying faithful to your systems in the past?
3. Who can support you in maintaining consistency in your goals?

Call to Action:

This week, choose one system to focus on and commit to staying consistent for seven days. Use a tracker to monitor your progress and reflect on how faithfulness in small actions brings peace and purpose.

Key Verse for the Week:
"Commit your work to the Lord, and your plans will be established."
– Proverbs 16:3

Chapter 9: The Power of Consistency – Staying Committed to Godly Systems

"Let us not grow weary in doing what is right, for we will reap at harvest time, if we do not give up."

(Galatians 6:9, NRSV)

Building systems in your life is only the first step. The true power of systems lies in consistency—faithfully following through day after day, even when the results are not immediately visible. Consistency is the bridge between intention and transformation.

In this chapter, we will explore the biblical principles of perseverance, the rewards of staying consistent, and practical strategies to maintain your systems over the long term.

Biblical Principles of Consistency

1. God is Faithful and Consistent

God's character is the ultimate example of consistency. His promises never fail, and His mercies are renewed daily.

"The steadfast love of the Lord never ceases, his mercies never come to an end; they are new every morning; great is your faithfulness" (Lamentations 3:22-23, NRSV).

As image-bearers of God, we are called to reflect His faithfulness in our actions.

2. Small Steps Lead to Big Results

Jesus taught that faithfulness in small things leads to greater responsibilities and rewards.

"Whoever is faithful in a very little is faithful also in much" (Luke 16:10, NRSV).

Small, consistent actions—praying daily, saving regularly, exercising faithfully—yield significant results over time.

3. Perseverance Produces Fruit

Paul reminds us that consistency, even in the face of challenges, produces lasting rewards.

"Let us not grow weary in doing what is right, for we will reap at harvest time, if we do not give up" (Galatians 6:9, NRSV).

Sticking to your systems, especially during difficult seasons, positions you for a future harvest of blessings.

The Rewards of Consistency

1. Spiritual Growth

Daily prayer, Bible study, and worship deepen your relationship with God. Over time, these practices transform your character and align your heart with His will.

"For it is God who is at work in you, enabling you both to will and to work for his good pleasure" (Philippians 2:13, NRSV).

2. Stability and Peace

Consistent routines create stability and reduce stress. Knowing your systems are in place frees you to focus on God's purposes.

"Great peace have those who love your law; nothing can make them stumble" (Psalm 119:165, NRSV).

3. Long-Term Success

Whether in finances, health, relationships, or spiritual growth, consistency leads to lasting success. Like a seed planted in good soil, faithful effort produces fruit in due season.

"The kingdom of God is as if someone would scatter seed on the ground... The earth produces of itself, first the stalk, then the head, then the full grain in the head" (Mark 4:26, 28, NRSV).

Obstacles to Consistency

1. Lack of Motivation

It's easy to lose motivation when results aren't immediate or the process feels monotonous.

"The spirit indeed is willing, but the flesh is weak" (Mark 14:38b, NRSV).

2. Distractions

Busyness, technology, and competing priorities often derail our focus.

"Martha, Martha, you are worried and distracted by many things; there is need of only one thing" (Luke 10:41-42, NRSV).

3. Discouragement

Setbacks and failures can tempt us to give up.

"Consider it nothing but joy, my brothers and sisters, whenever you fall into various trials, because you know that the testing of your faith produces endurance" (James 1:2-3, NRSV).

Strategies for Staying Consistent

1. Keep Your "Why" in Mind

Remind yourself why the system matters. Whether it's honoring God, improving your health, or strengthening a relationship, keeping your "why" in focus motivates you to stay on track.

"Whatever you do, do everything for the glory of God" (1 Corinthians 10:31, NRSV).

2. Start Small and Build Momentum

It's better to start with small, manageable steps than to take on too much and burn out. Success in one area builds confidence to tackle others.

3. Set a Schedule

Consistency thrives on routine. Establish a specific time for your daily or weekly practices. For example:

- Morning prayer and Bible study.
- Weekly family meetings.
- Monthly financial reviews.

"For everything there is a season, and a time for every matter under heaven" (Ecclesiastes 3:1, NRSV).

4. Track Your Progress

Use journals, apps, or calendars to monitor your consistency. Celebrate small victories and acknowledge growth over time.

5. Find Accountability

Share your goals with a trusted friend, mentor, or group. Accountability partners encourage you to stay consistent and provide support when challenges arise.

"Therefore encourage one another and build up each other, as indeed you are doing" (1 Thessalonians 5:11, NRSV).

Reflection: How Consistent Are You?

Take a moment to evaluate your consistency. Ask yourself:

1. **Which systems in my life are working well because of consistent effort?**
2. **What areas of inconsistency need attention?**
3. **What steps can I take to stay faithful to the systems God has called me to implement?**

Action Steps for Chapter 9

1. **Identify One Area to Improve:**
   Choose one system—spiritual, financial, relational, or physical—and commit to practicing it consistently this week.

2. **Set a Routine:**
   Establish a specific time and method for your chosen practice. For example:

   - Pray and read Scripture for 15 minutes each morning.
   - Walk for 20 minutes three times this week.
3. **Track Your Progress:**
   Write down each day's successes and challenges. Celebrate even small improvements.

4. **Invite Accountability:**
   Share your goal with someone you trust and ask them to check in with you regularly.

Conclusion: Faithfulness Brings the Harvest

Consistency is not about perfection but persistence. By staying faithful to the systems God has led you to build, you align your life with His principles and position yourself for blessing. Even when progress feels slow, trust that your faithfulness is sowing seeds for a harvest.

"The one who sows to the Spirit will reap eternal life from the Spirit. So let us not grow weary in doing what is right, for we will reap at harvest time, if we do not give up" (Galatians 6:8-9, NRSV).

In the next chapter, we will explore how to share and multiply the systems you've built, teaching others how to live with intention and align their lives with God's purposes.

Chapter 10: Teaching and Multiplying Systems – Empowering Others to Live Intentionally

"Go therefore and make disciples of all nations, baptizing them in the name of the Father and of the Son and of the Holy Spirit, and teaching them to obey everything that I have commanded you."

(Matthew 28:19-20a, NRSV)

When we implement systems that align with God's order, they not only bless our lives but also position us to bless others. Jesus modeled this principle by creating systems for discipling His followers and empowering them to carry His mission forward. Teaching and multiplying systems are acts of stewardship and love, equipping others to live intentionally and fulfill their God-given purposes.

In this chapter, we will explore how to share the systems you've built with others, teach them to create their own, and inspire a legacy of growth and transformation.

Biblical Principles for Teaching and Multiplying Systems

1. Discipleship is a System

Jesus' ministry was intentional and systematic. He invested deeply in 12 disciples, teaching them God's principles and equipping them to carry the message forward.

"Then he appointed twelve, whom he also named apostles, to be with him, and to be sent out to proclaim the message" (Mark 3:14, NRSV).

This relational system ensured that His teachings would multiply across generations.

2. Teaching Brings Transformation

God's truth is meant to be shared, and teaching is a critical part of equipping others for transformation.

"All scripture is inspired by God and is useful for teaching, for reproof, for correction, and for training in righteousness, so that everyone who belongs to God may be proficient, equipped for every good work" (2 Timothy 3:16-17, NRSV).

Teaching systems rooted in biblical principles helps others grow in wisdom, discipline, and purpose.

3. Empower Others to Take Ownership

Paul encouraged Timothy to entrust God's teachings to faithful people who could continue the work:

"What you have heard from me through many witnesses entrust to faithful people who will be able to teach others as well" (2 Timothy 2:2, NRSV).

Multiplying systems means equipping others to take ownership of their growth and influence.

4. Use the Power of Example

Jesus taught through both words and actions. His life was the model for His disciples to follow.

"For I have set you an example, that you also should do as I have done to you" (John 13:15, NRSV).

Leading by example inspires trust and demonstrates the effectiveness of the systems you share.

Steps for Teaching and Multiplying Systems

Step 1: Live the System Consistently

Before you can teach others, you must model the system in your own life. People are inspired by what they see, not just what they hear. Ask yourself:

- Am I consistently practicing the systems I've built?
- Do my actions reflect the values and principles I teach?

"Keep on doing the things that you have learned and received and heard and seen in me, and the God of peace will be with you" (Philippians 4:9, NRSV).

Step 2: Simplify and Explain

When teaching systems to others, simplicity is key. Break down the system into clear, actionable steps:

- **Describe the Purpose:** Why is this system important?
- **Explain the Components:** What are the key steps or elements?
- **Demonstrate the Process:** Show how the system works in real life.

For example:

- **Spiritual System:** Teach someone how to establish a daily quiet time by outlining steps like setting a specific time, choosing a Scripture reading plan, and journaling prayers.

- **Financial System:** Guide a friend in creating a budget by explaining categories, tracking expenses, and setting savings goals.

Step 3: Provide Tools and Resources

Equip others with the tools they need to succeed. This may include:

- Templates or worksheets.

- Recommended books, apps, or videos.

- Regular check-ins or accountability meetings.

"My people are destroyed for lack of knowledge" (Hosea 4:6a, NRSV).

Providing resources ensures that those you teach are set up for success.

Step 4: Encourage Ownership and Accountability

Empower others to take ownership of their systems. Encourage them to:

- Adapt the system to fit their unique needs and circumstances.

- Set specific goals and track their progress.

- Share their journey with an accountability partner.

Accountability fosters growth and ensures that the system becomes a sustainable part of their lives.

Step 5: Inspire Multiplication

Encourage those you teach to pass on what they've learned to others. This creates a ripple effect of transformation.

"The things you have prepared, whose will they be?" (Luke 12:20b, NRSV).

Teaching others to teach ensures that the principles and systems you've shared continue to bear fruit long after your involvement.

Practical Examples of Multiplying Systems

1. Family Discipleship

Teach your children or loved ones the importance of systems for spiritual growth, financial stewardship, and healthy habits. Create family routines like:

- Daily devotions or prayer time.
- Weekly family meetings to discuss schedules and goals.
- Shared chores and responsibilities to build teamwork and accountability.

2. Mentorship

Invest in someone's growth by sharing your systems for success. For example:

- Guide a young professional in time management or goal setting.
- Help a new believer establish spiritual disciplines.

3. Community Leadership

If you lead a small group, ministry, or organization, implement systems to ensure effectiveness and sustainability. Examples include:

- Creating a system for onboarding new members.
- Developing a schedule for teaching or serving.

Reflection: How Are You Sharing and Multiplying?

Take a moment to reflect on your influence. Ask yourself:

1. **Am I living the systems I want to teach?**
2. **Who in my life could benefit from learning these systems?**
3. **How can I empower others to multiply these principles in their own lives?**

Action Steps for Chapter 10

1. **Choose One System to Share:**
   Identify a system you've successfully implemented—spiritual, financial, relational, or physical—and decide who you can teach it to.
2. **Prepare a Simple Teaching Plan:**
   Break the system into clear steps and gather any tools or resources needed.
3. **Teach and Encourage:**
   Schedule a time to share the system with someone. Follow up regularly to provide support and encouragement.
4. **Inspire Multiplication:**
   Challenge the person you've taught to pass on what they've learned to someone else.

Conclusion: A Legacy of Transformation

Teaching and multiplying systems is an act of obedience and love, reflecting God's desire for growth and flourishing. By sharing the systems you've built, you empower others to live intentionally, honor God, and bless those around them. This legacy of transformation echoes far beyond your own life, creating a ripple effect for generations to come.

"The things you have heard from me... entrust to faithful people who will be able to teach others also" (2 Timothy 2:2, NRSV).

As we conclude this journey through the principles of godly systems, remember that your faithfulness to build, sustain, and share these systems aligns you with God's divine order and positions you to experience His abundant blessings.

SUMMARY

From the beginning, God's design has reflected order, purpose, and intentionality. In this book, we have explored how the systems God established in creation, Scripture, and human relationships provide a framework for living a life aligned with His will. These systems—spiritual, financial, relational, physical, and communicative—are not just practical tools but sacred pathways that bring peace, abundance, and fulfillment.

The key principles of this book include:

1. **God is a God of Systems:** Everything in creation, from the cosmos to the human body, operates through interconnected systems that reflect His wisdom and order.
2. **Systems Require Discipline and Intentionality:** Building and maintaining systems takes effort, but the rewards include stability, growth, and alignment with God's purposes.
3. **Consistency is Key:** Faithful adherence to systems transforms small daily actions into long-term success and spiritual fruitfulness.
4. **Multiplying Systems Blesses Others:** Sharing and teaching these systems empowers others to live intentionally and creates a ripple effect of transformation.

As you reflect on this journey, remember that God's systems are designed to bless and equip you for every good work. By embracing divine order in your life, you position yourself to experience His peace, power, and provision.

Final Reflection

Take time to pray and seek God's guidance as you implement and refine the systems in your life. Ask Him to reveal areas of disorder and show you how to align them with His principles. Commit to consistency, remain open to growth, and encourage others to join you in living a life of divine order.

"Commit your work to the Lord, and your plans will be established" (Proverbs 16:3, NRSV).

Made in the USA
Middletown, DE
31 March 2025

73466631R00037